ISBN: 978-1-7372877-0-4 (hardcover)
ISBN: 978-1-7372877-1-1 (ebook)

Library of Congress Control Number: 2021910647

Headshots for jacket design by Shane Stewart
Front cover Illustration by Faith Henke
Book design by Faith Henke and Josh Pedersen

First Edition

First printing August 2021

Paragon Press Inc.
2532 South 3270 West
Salt Lake City, Utah 84119

Printed in the United States of America

TO ALL PARENTS, WHO DESPiTE VAST DiFFERENCES CHOSE *LOVE* OVER ALL ELSE.

TO ALL THOSE WHO CAME BEFORE ME, PAViNG THE WAY BY *PROUDLY* BEiNG THEMSELVES.

AND FiNALLY, TO ALL THE FRiENDS WHO WERE KiND BEFORE iT WAS COOL TO HAVE A QUEER FRiEND.

OUT OF 8 BILLION HUMANS ON EARTH—YOU'RE CUSTOM BUILT. THE ONLY ONE ON THE PLANET TO TAKE LIFE TO THE HILT!

AND NOW THAT

WE'VE OPENED THIS

BOOK AND BEGUN,

YOU SHOULD KNOW

THAT THIS NARRATIVE

IS FOR EVERYONE.

LET US START THiS WAY,
HUMANS ARE NOT ALWAYS KiND —
SOMETiMES THEY'RE JUST
NOT iN THEiR

RiGHT
MiND.

THEY CAN BRING PAIN AND SADNESS,
EVEN MAKE YOU FEEL DUMB.

BUT HOW IS THIS POSSIBLE?
YOU'RE UNIQUE!

ONE OF ONE!

NOT TO STRESS,
NOT TO WORRY,
FOR THEY ARE QUITE WRONG.
NO MATTER THEIR WORDS,
YOU WILL
ALWAYS BELONG,

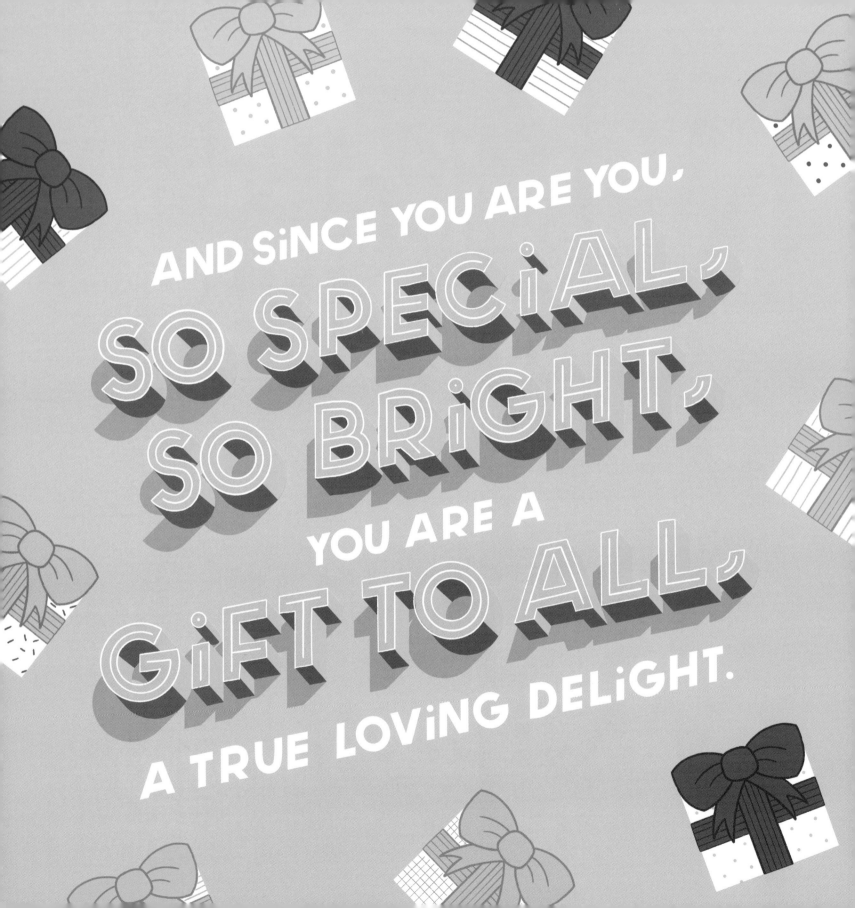

AND SINCE YOU ARE YOU,

SO SPECIAL,

SO BRIGHT,

YOU ARE A

GIFT TO ALL,

A TRUE LOVING DELIGHT.

AT FIRST YOU MIGHT
FEEL YOU'VE BEEN GIVEN
A BURDEN TO BEAR.
THAT YOU HAVE SECRETS,
OR CONFUSION YOU
DON'T QUITE KNOW
HOW TO SHARE.

YOU MAY FEEL DiFFERENT,
DON'T FORGET, THAT'S OKAY.
I THiNK YOU WERE GiVEN A STAR
FROM THE VAST MiLKY WAY!

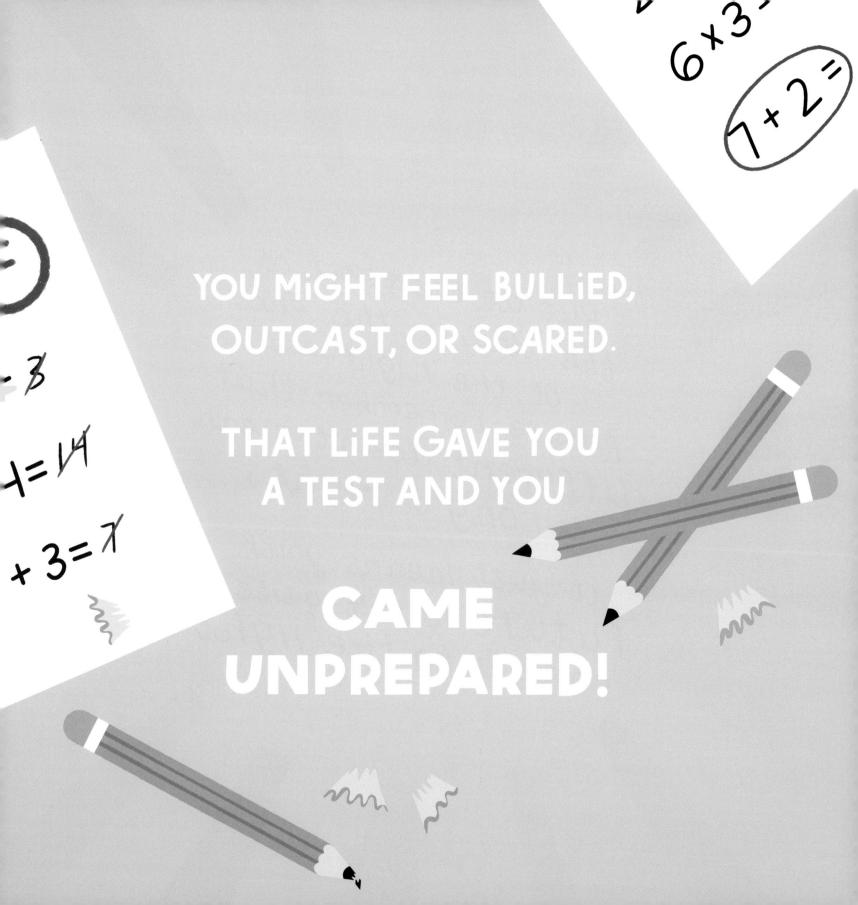

YOU MiGHT FEEL BULLiED, OUTCAST, OR SCARED.

THAT LiFE GAVE YOU A TEST AND YOU

CAME UNPREPARED!

But at the start of the day, or the end of the night—

please remember that different doesn't mean wrong or right,

it just means your future hasn't quite come into the light.

YOU MAY HAVE
LIKED TOYS THAT WERE
DIFFERENT FROM PEERS.

MAYBE SHAMED FOR
YOUR FEELINGS,
IT WAS JUST
SO UNCLEAR.

AS YOU GET OLDER
YOUR FEELINGS GET STRONGER—
YET, YOU STILL CAN'T EXPLAIN.

LIKE WHEN THE WEATHER
FORECASTS SUN,
AND ALL YOU GET IS RAIN.

THOSE FEELiNGS
ARE NOT BAD.
THEY MAKE YOU UNiQUE.

DON'T EVER LET ANYONE
MAKE YOU FEEL LESS,
CALL YOU NAMES
OR TELL YOU
YOU'RE WEAK. #@!

WHEN IT'S TIME,
YOU MAY WANT TO
SHARE HOW YOU FEEL.

NO NEED TO RUSH.
THEY'RE YOURS AND
YOU KNOW
THEY'RE REAL.

YOU MAY LiVE iN A PLACE WHERE
iT FEELS SAFE TO SAY WHAT YOU LiKE—
OR, PERHAPS YOU DO NOT, AND YOU'RE
AFRAiD OF EMBARRASSMENT AND DiSLiKE.

BUT... YOU KNOW
DEEP DOWN,

HOW GOOD iT FEELS
TO BE TRUE,

ESPECiALLY WHEN YOU
LOOK iN THE MiRROR

AND THE MiRROR
SMiLES BACK AT YOU.

here are
some wisdoms—
some old and
some new,

that could
possibly help
with a hard decision
or two.

PAUSE FOR A MOMENT
AND THINK OF YOUR KIN,
THE ONES THAT YOU LOVE,
THE FAMILY YOU'RE IN.

THINK OF YOUR PARENTS,
THINK OF THE SHOES THEY WALK IN.

Most likely they don't know how you feel—you feel—suspicions, maybe so? But you are the only one that can truthfully let them know.

YOU MAY NOT HAVE THE OPTiON
TO DO SO—THAT iS PERFECTLY FiNE!

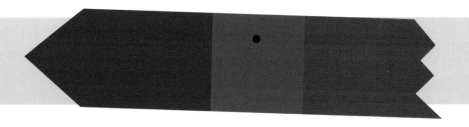

REMEMBER, THESE ARE JUST NOTES;

NOT RULES CARVED iNTO A SiGN.

THINGS MIGHT NOT HAPPEN THE WAY YOU EXPECTED.
THAT'S WHY YOU DON'T WANT HOLIDAYS CONNECTED.

SAVE YOURSELF THE STRIFE, AND PICK A DATE
THAT AFFECTS ONLY YOUR LIFE!

THiRD, FOR THiS SPECiAL TALK,
LET FRiENDS SiT THiS ONE OUT,

i PROMiSE YOU'VE GOT THiS,
100%—NO DOUBT.

GIVE YOUR PARENTS
TIME TO HEAR

AND REACT TO WHAT
YOU HAVE SAID—

TO PROCESS AND THINK,

"WHAT'S
NEXT?

WHAT'S
AHEAD?"

THIS WON'T BE EASY, IT WOULD BE MUCH MORE COMFORTABLE UNSAID. BUT REMEMBER, UNLIKE YOU, THEY HAVEN'T HAD NUMEROUS NIGHTS FILLED WITH ANXIETY AND DREAD.

FOR YOU HAVE HAD YEARS OF
TURMOIL AND ACHE,
TURBULENT WAVES
ON A CALM SUMMER LAKE.

YOU'VE RELEASED THE REAL YOU.
"THIS IS WHO I AM!"
WATER RELEASED FROM
A CONFINING DAM.

but, you did it!

YOU SAID IT!

YOU NEED ONLY ONCE!

now all you desire is simple

ACCEPTANCE.

THiS iS AS BRAVE AS YOU'VE BEEN.

YOU SHOULD BE PROUD!

FEEL RELiEF, FEEL ENDOWED!

THESE FEELINGS RUN DEEP
AND HAVE CAUSED MUCH SORROW,
BUT COMING OUT GIVES YOU
HOPE OF A BETTER TOMORROW,

FEEL BRAVE, YOU DID IT!
A TREK HARDER THAN KILIMANJARO!

AFTER CAN BE HARD.
iT CAN TAKE
TiME FOR SOME
TO ADJUST.

iF THERE iS
ANGER OR MEANNESS,
TAKE A MiNUTE;
WALK AWAY iF
YOU MUST.

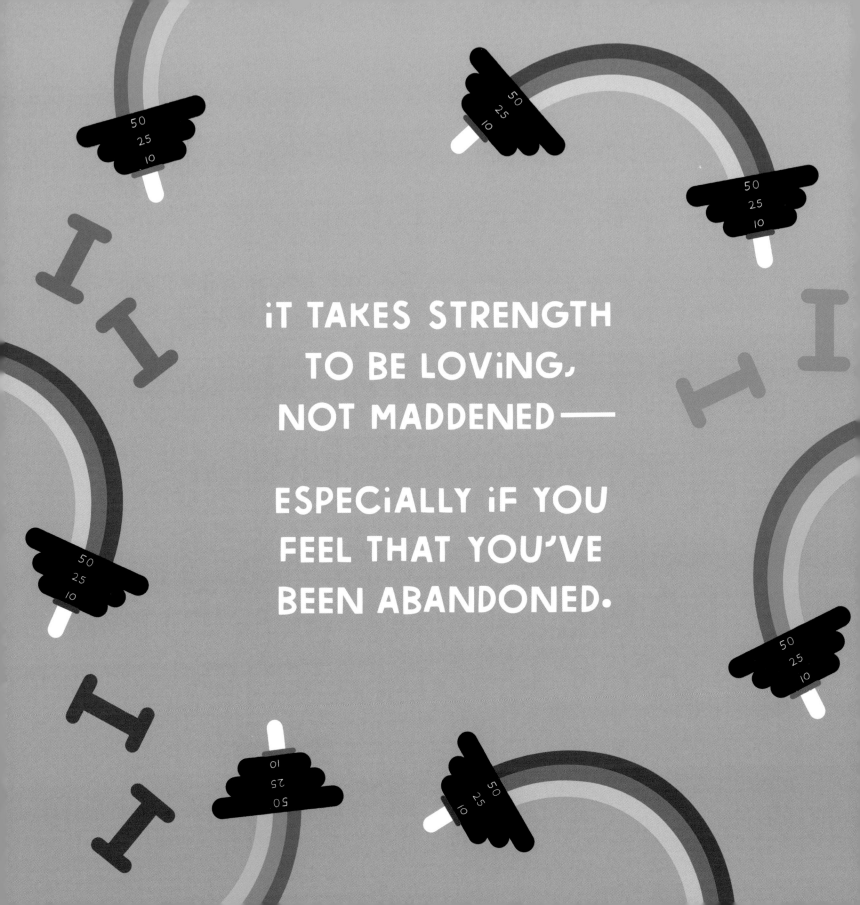

IT TAKES STRENGTH
TO BE LOVING,
NOT MADDENED—

ESPECIALLY IF YOU
FEEL THAT YOU'VE
BEEN ABANDONED.

FOR THOSE AROUND
YOU WHO DON'T
UNDERSTAND,

LET THEM KNOW
THAT YOU LOVE THEM,
THEN TAKE PRIDE AND
EXPAND!

iT'S UNLiKELY THAT
ONE PERSON WiLL EVER
BE LOVED BY ALL.

BUT YOU CAN
Love OTHERS,

LOVE YOU, HAVE COURAGE
AND STAND TALL.

FOR YOU ARE NO
DiFFERENT THAN BEFORE.
JUST THE BATTLE
iNSiDE YOU LiVES ON
NO MORE!

YOU ARE THE SAME BRAVE HUMAN YOU ALWAYS HAVE BEEN!

YOU ARE THE SAME

BRAVE
HUMAN

JUST
OUT,

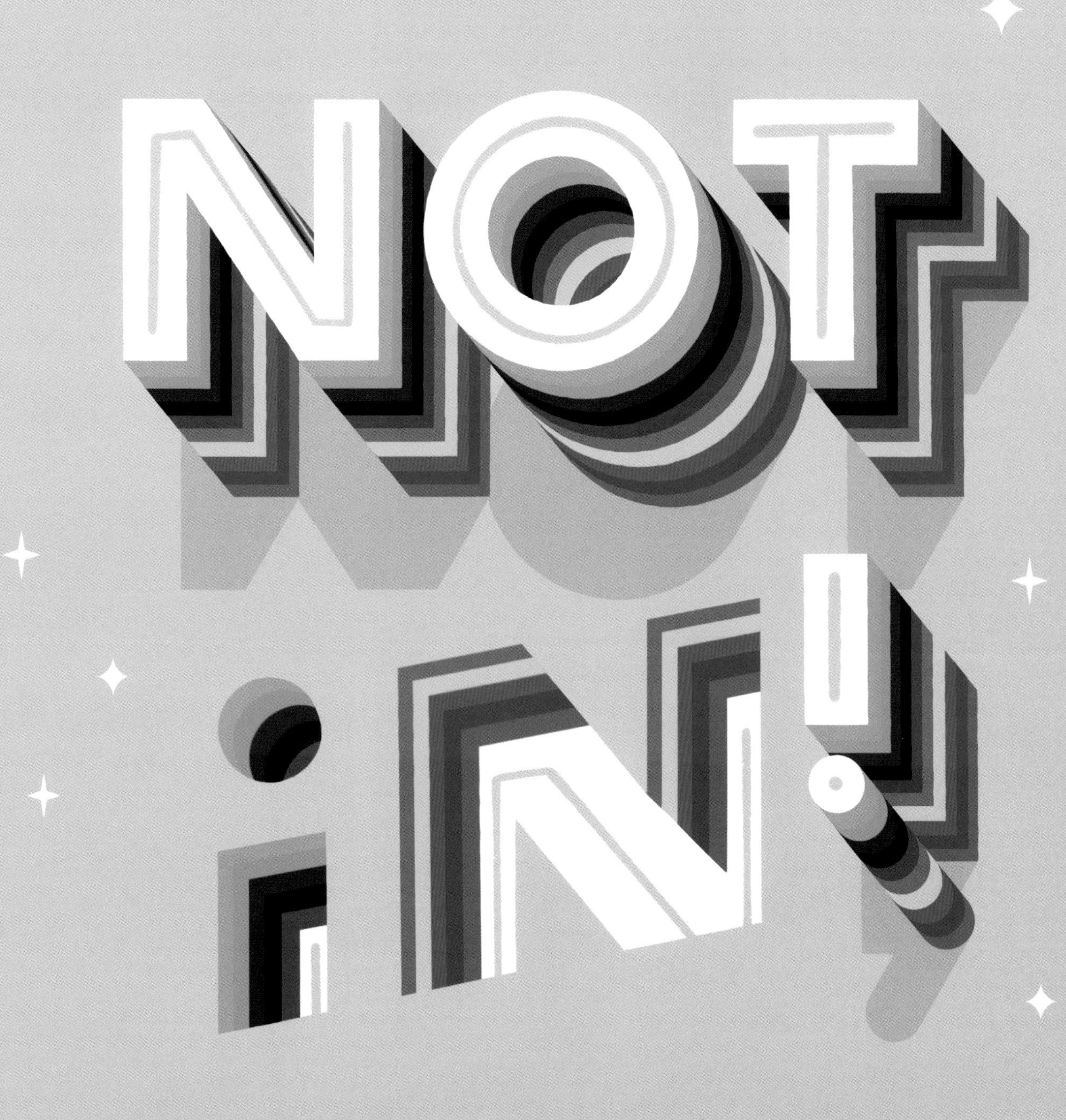
NOT
iN!